Listening

Truth

Expression

Vishuddha

Air

Story

Talk

Clarity

Throat

Self-expression

Blue

Voice

speech

Joke

song

Communication

Throat Chakra Adventures:

Speaking Truth
with
Aquamarine and Topaz

Volume 5

By: K.C. Gold

"This book is dedicated to you.
Speak your truth."

Northern Lights Publishing LLC.

https://northernlightskids.com/

Hello, I am Aquamarine
With Topaz by my side,
We are spinning energy particles,
Where your communication resides.

We are located at the base
of your throat,
Throat Chakra is what they
call us,
But we don't like to gloat.

We are the energy force
That helps you speak your
truth,
With clarity and conviction,
Only the best for you.

We are here to have fun
And lend a hand,
But sometimes we need help,
We need your command.

If you
struggle
to
express,

Or
your
thoughts
you can't find,

It means we're unbalanced,
Our spin's in a bind.

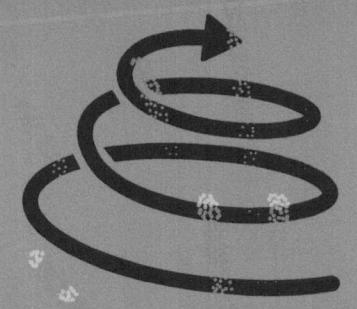

To get us spinning right,
741 times plus two,
Here's what you can do,
These options are for you.

Hertz Meter

1 Hertz (Hz) = 1 Spin Per Second

741Hz

Sweet sounds delight us,
'G' pitch we adore,
With its melody so pure,
We'll spin even more.

Dance and sway your neck,
Take a graceful bow,
Feel our whirl begin,
As you move and allow.

Dress in shades of blue,
It suits you through and through,
Feel the calming hue,
As we spin just for you.

Enjoy a tasty treat,

From the Earth's fertile seat,

Watch us dance and greet,

In a spin so sweet.

Sit in a quiet place,
Surrounded by the color blue,
Give these mantras a try,
Choose the best for you.

"I speak my truth,
Like a melody so clear,
Expressing myself,
I have no fear."

"Words of success,
Words of might,
I speak with power,
Shining so bright."

"Listen and learn
before I speak,
Understanding first,
Makes me unique."

"I speak my truth,
Clear and strong,
Like a drumbeat in a
catchy song."

And when you feel your voice start to ignite,

You will know that you chose the mantra for you that is right.

A sky of blue in your
throat's gentle sway,
Where words find their
voice,
In wisdom's array.

With truth and expression,
Let your voice be heard clear,
Throat Chakra's melody is sweet to the ear!

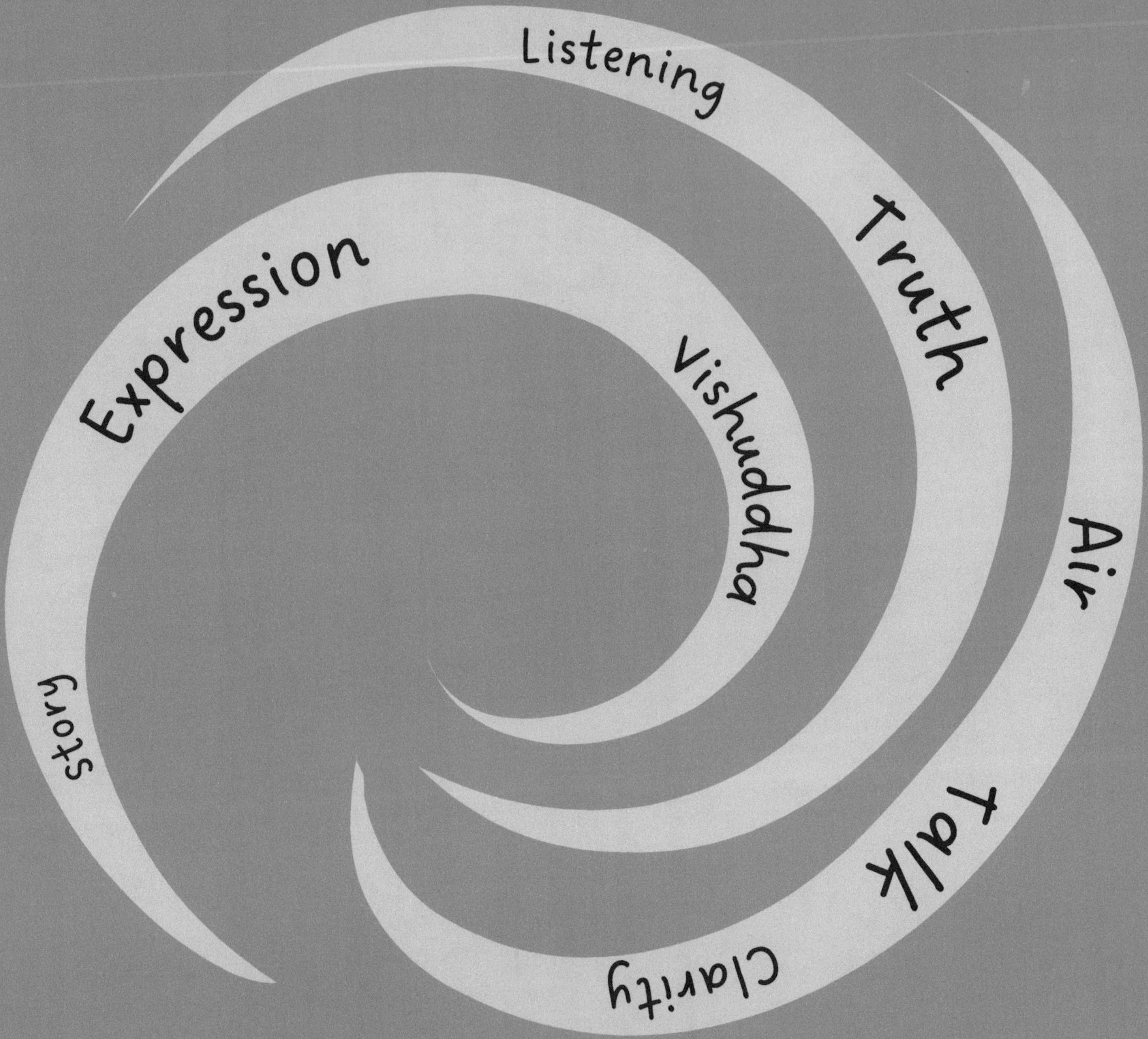

Listening

Truth

Air

Talk

Clarity

Vishuddha

Expression

Story

Dear Reader,

Thank you for taking the time to read this book. If you found value in it, I would be incredibly grateful if you could take a few moments to leave a review. Your feedback not only helps me improve but also aids other readers in discovering books they might enjoy.

Thank you once again for your support and for being a part of this adventure!

Warm regards,
K.C. Gold

Amazon

Northern Lights
Publishing

Speak your truth.